To: _____

From: _____

SMILE

Linda Maron

Written by Peter Stein

**Andrews McMeel
Publishing**

Kansas City

05 06 07 08 09 TWP 10 9 8 7 6 5 4 3 2 1

ISBN: 0-7407-5032-1

Library of Congress Control Number: 2004111163

SMILE

This is a little book
about smiling.

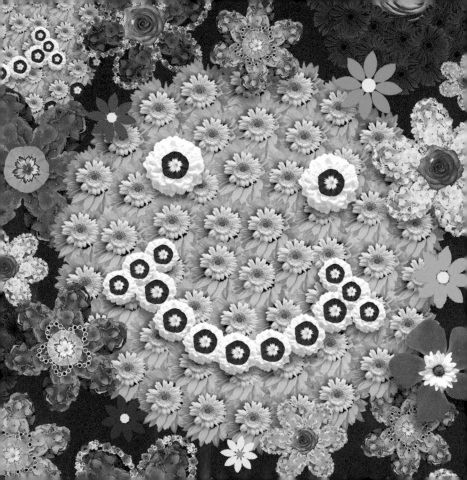

$\mathcal{Y}$esterday is no more.
Tomorrow is
impossible to touch.
There's a moment—
right here, right now.
It's calling your name.

So smile,

because nurturing
the part of yourself
that makes you happy
is smart.

You know why?

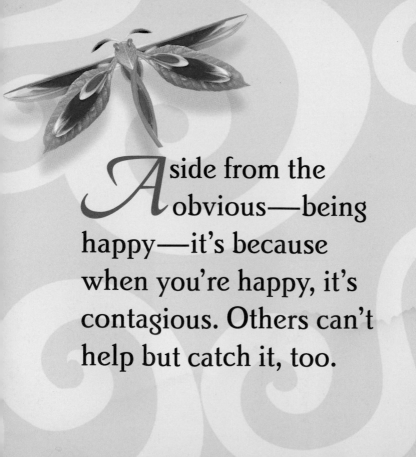

$\mathcal{A}$ side from the obvious—being happy—it's because when you're happy, it's contagious. Others can't help but catch it, too.

*A*nd as we all learned once upon a time: It's nice to share.

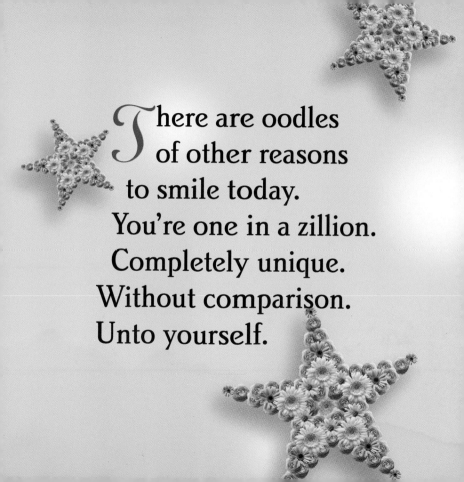

There are oodles
of other reasons
to smile today.
You're one in a zillion.
Completely unique.
Without comparison.
Unto yourself.

You're lovely. Cool. Funny. Creative. Nice. And a snappy dresser, too.

$\mathcal{I}$n short,
you're simply . . .

*J*ust in case you need another reason to smile—consider the happiness friends bring. A good friend knows where you're coming from, knows where you've been, and is there for you, 24/7.

So smile,

because even though life
sometimes rains on our
parade (or picnic,
or campground, or
croquet tournament),

without the storms,
we'd never have the
outrageous beauty
of rainbows.

*B*esides, when you're in the eye of the storm, sometimes that's the best place to make waves!

And if you've been swimming upstream, maybe you're just building strength for a big change in your life.

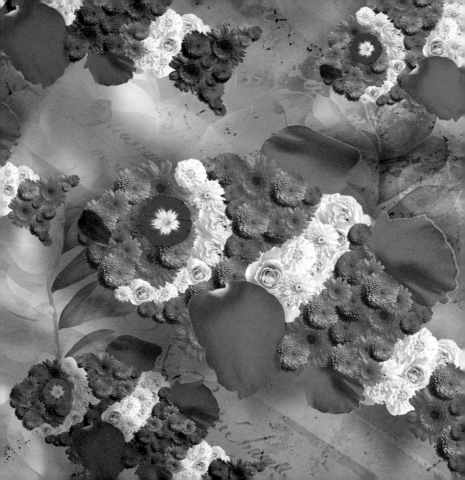

We all know change is hard work. And hard work should be rewarded . . . with treats! The world is full of riches created simply to give you pleasure. Lots and lots of pleasure. It is wise indeed to indulge.

Often!

Sure, clichés are everywhere. Here's a biggie: "You can be as happy as you decide to be." And it just happens to be true!

Sometimes you can make a wrong turn and walk through the right door.

And sometimes gladness just falls—thump!—right into your lap, because you realize simply being alive is a profound gift, waiting to be unwrapped.

These are the times to dance to the sunset . . . sing with the birds . . . shout out your own personal theme song.

So smile,

because right now,
somebody thinks you're
very . . .

Somebody is there
when you're up or
down . . . or in between.

And somebody
cares about you.
A lot.

So whether you're far from home on a wild adventure, figuring out what it's all about . . .

or hanging around
the house,

*B*ecause there are too many reasons not to . . . and because it looks beautiful on you.